Pebble®

Bill Gates

Microsoft®

by Christopher L. Harbo

Consulting Editor: Gail Saunders-Smith, PhD

Consultant: Miles Smayling, PhD
Professor of Management
Minnesota State University, Mankato

CAPSTONE PRESS
a capstone imprint

Pebble Books are published by Capstone Press,
1710 Roe Crest Drive, North Mankato, Minnesota 56003
www.capstonepub.com

Library of Congress Cataloging-in-Publication Data
Harbo, Christopher L.
Bill Gates / by Christopher L. Harbo.
pages cm. — (Pebble books. Business leaders)
Includes bibliographical references and index.
Summary: "Simple text and photographs present the life of Bill Gates, founder of Microsoft"—
Provided by publisher.
Audience: Age 4 to 8.
Audience: Grade K to 3.
ISBN 978-1-4765-9641-9 (library binding)
ISBN 978-1-4765-9645-7 (paperback)
ISBN 978-1-4765-9649-5 (eBook PDF)
1. Gates, Bill, 1955—Juvenile literature. 2. Businessmen—United States—Biography—Juvenile
literature. 3. Success in business—Juvenile literature. 4. Computer software industry—United
States—History—Juvenile literature. 5. Microsoft Corporation—History—Juvenile literature. 6.
Bill & Melinda Gates Foundation—History—Juvenile literature. I. Title.
HD9696.2.U62G3747 2013
338.7'61004092—dc23
[B]   2013035614

Note to Parents and Teachers

The Business Leaders set supports national social studies standards
related to people, places, and environments. This book describes
and illustrates Bill Gates. The images support early readers in
understanding the text. The repetition of words and phrases helps
early readers learn new words. This book also introduces early
readers to subject-specific vocabulary words, which are defined
in the Glossary section. Early readers may need assistance to read
some words and to use the Table of Contents, Glossary, Read More,
Internet Sites, and Index sections of the book.

Printed in the United States of America in North Mankato, Minnesota.
092013   007764CGS14

Table of Contents

Early Years 5
Building Microsoft 9
Work and Family 15
Giving Back. 19

Glossary 22
Critical Thinking Using the
Common Core 22
Read More 23
Internet Sites. 23
Index 24

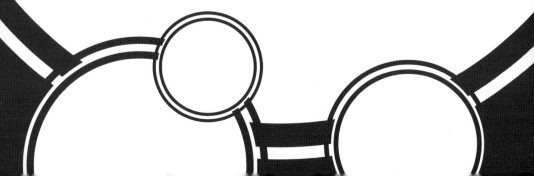

Seattle, Washington

1955

born in
Washington

Early Years

Computer software inventor Bill Gates was born October 28, 1955, in Seattle, Washington. As a child he enjoyed board games. Bill also loved math and science.

Paul Allen and Bill Gates at Lakeside School in Seattle

1955

born in
Washington

At age 13, Bill started using a new computer at his school. He and his friend Paul Allen wrote programs to run on it. In high school Bill and Paul sold software to companies.

Bill and Paul in 1984

1955

1975

born in
Washington

starts company that
becomes Microsoft

Building Microsoft

In 1975 Bill and Paul started their own business. It became known as Microsoft. Their company began making software for personal computers (PCs).

Bill in 1986

1955
born in
Washington

1975
starts company that
becomes Microsoft

1985
releases
Windows 1.0

In 1985 Microsoft came out with Windows 1.0. This allowed people to control PCs with a mouse. Within a few years, most PCs came with Windows software. Bill's success made him a billionaire.

Bill in 1989

1955
1975
1985

12   born in
Washington

starts company that
becomes Microsoft

releases
Windows 1.0

Microsoft became the world's largest software company. Bill asked his employees to think up bigger ideas. In 1989 his company released Microsoft Office. It helped businesses get work done faster.

Bill and Melinda in 1998

1955
born in
Washington

1975
starts company that
becomes Microsoft

1985
releases
Windows 1.0

1994
marries
Melinda French

Work and Family

In 1989 Bill met Melinda French. She was an employee at Microsoft. Melinda liked Bill's sense of humor. They shared many interests. In 1994 they got married in Hawaii.

1955
born in
Washington

1975
starts company that
becomes Microsoft

1985
releases
Windows 1.0

1994
marries
Melinda French

16

Bill and Melinda were busy in the mid-1990s. Microsoft developed Internet Explorer in 1995. This program helped people search the Internet. At home, Bill and Melinda started a family. Their first of three children was born in 1996.

Bill and Melinda visit villages in India for their foundation.

1955
born in
Washington

1975
starts company that
becomes Microsoft

1985
releases
Windows 1.0

1994
marries
Melinda French

Giving Back

Bill and Melinda wanted to help others. In 2000 they started the Bill and Melinda Gates Foundation. It gives about $2 billion each year to improve education and health care around the world.

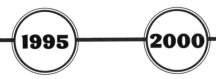

1995
releases
Internet Explorer

2000
starts the Bill and Melinda
Gates Foundation

1955
1975
1985
1994

20   born in   starts company that   releases   marries
Washington   becomes Microsoft   Windows 1.0   Melinda French

In 2005 *Time* magazine named Bill and Melinda "Persons of the Year." In 2008 Bill left Microsoft. But he still works for his foundation. He wants to make life better for people all over the world.

1995
releases
Internet Explorer

2000
starts the Bill and Melinda
Gates Foundation

2005
wins "Persons of
the Year" honor

2008
leaves
Microsoft

Glossary

billionaire—someone who has $1 billion or more

Internet—a system that connects computers all over the world

inventor—a person who thinks of and creates something new; the new item is his or her invention

program—a series of step-by-step instructions that tells a computer what to do

software—the programs used by a computer

Critical Thinking Using the Common Core

1. Look at the photo on page 16. What is happening in this picture? What clues did you use from the photo to help you find your answer? (Craft and Structure)

2. Microsoft has developed computer programs, like Microsoft Office and Internet Explorer. Using the text, describe two ways these programs have helped people use computers. Tell about a program you have used on a computer. (Integration of Knowledge and Ideas)

Read More

Demuth, Patricia. *Who Is Bill Gates?* New York: Grosset & Dunlap, 2013.

Gregory, Josh. *Bill and Melinda Gates.* A True Book. New York: Children's Press, 2013.

Musolf, Nell. *The Story of Microsoft.* Built for Success. Mankato, Minn.: Creative Education, 2009.

Internet Sites

FactHound offers a safe, fun way to find Internet sites related to this book. All of the sites on FactHound have been researched by our staff.

Here's all you do:

Visit *www.facthound.com*

Type in this code: 9781476596419

Check out projects, games and lots more at
www.capstonekids.com

Index

Allen, Paul, 7, 9
Bill and Melinda Gates
  Foundation, 19, 21
birth, 5
companies, 7, 9, 13
computers, 5, 7, 9, 11
family, 17
Gates, Melinda, 15, 17,
  19, 21
Internet Explorer, 17

marriage, 15
Microsoft, 9, 11, 13, 15, 17,
  21
personal computers (PCs),
  9, 11
Seattle, Washington, 5
software, 5, 7, 9, 11, 13
"Persons of the Year", 21
Windows, 11

Word Count: 279
Grade: 1
Early-Intervention Level: 24

Editorial Credits

Michelle Hasselius, editor; Lori Bye, designer; Tracy Cummins, media researcher;
Jennifer Walker, production specialist

Photo Credits

ageFOTOSTOCK: © Year book library, 6; Corbis: Doug Wilson, 8; Dreamstime: © St3fano,
cover; Flickr: The Alieness Gisela Giardino, 20; Getty Images: Jeff Christensen, 14, Joe
McNally, 10, Luc Novovitch, 12, STRDEL/AFP, 18; Newscom: Paul J. RICHARDS/Agence
France Presse, 16; Shutterstock: Godruma, cover background, Peteri, 1, Rigucci, 4